MINORITY AND WOMEN BUSINESS ENTERPRISE

CERTIFICATION LEVELS PLAYING FIELD

PAMELA WILLIAMSON Ph.D

WITH CO-AUTHOR ROBIN BILLUPS

Published By Social Marketing Firm

Email: contact@socialmarketingfirm.co

Website: www.asmf.co

ISBN: 978-0615680804

Printed in the United States of America

CONTENTS

ROI For Using Diverse Suppliers 1

What Is A Minority Business Enterprise 3

What Is A Women Business Enterprise 4

Minority Business Enterprises By The Numbers 5

Women Business Enterprises By The Numbers 7

What Is Minority Certification 9

National Minority Supplier Development Council 10

United States Small Business Administration 11

HUB Zone 12

Section 8(a) Business Development Program 14

How To Become Women-Owned Certified 16

Small Business Association 18

Problems 19

Increase Your Opportunity for Success 22

Testimonials 25

ROI FOR USING DIVERSE SUPPLIERS

Supplier diversity is a business initiative that encourages the use of minority and women-owned business enterprises as suppliers. Supplier diversity is a practice of sourcing products and services from previously under-used suppliers. In doing so, businesses and corporations help sustain and transform their supply chain to reflect the demographics of the community in which they operate.

Historically, minority and women-owned businesses have been underutilized, but today, minority and women-owned businesses are among the fastest-growing segments of the American economy. In fact, minority-owned businesses generate an estimated $495 billion in annual revenue and employ nearly 4 million workers according to a 1997 report by the United States Small Business Administration. A similar report from the Center For Women Business Research found that women-owned businesses generate $2.5 trillion in annual sales and employ about 19 million people.

For this reason, in the early 21st century, more and more businesses and companies are turning to diverse suppliers for goods and services. Despite social constructs that sometimes put diverse suppliers at a disadvantage, companies have begun to identify the value of contracting and working with diverse suppliers. Previously, supplier diversity programs focused on the social ramifications of increasing supplier diversity. However, today's diversity programs are demonstrating that working with diverse suppliers can yield a high return on investment.

Supplier diversity can enhance a business' competitiveness while

1

increasing flexibility and innovation. It can also lead to cost savings, a higher quality of goods, and higher efficiency. Since supplier diversity programs improve an enterprise's public image, embracing supplier diversity will increase an enterprise's customer base and ultimately their bottom line. As a whole, embracing supplier diversity can help reduce the cost of an enterprise's procurement portfolio, expand an enterprises influence in various markets, and enhance an enterprises ability to innovate.

WHAT IS A MINORITY BUSINESS ENTERPRISE

A minority-owned business is a phrase used to describe a for-profit proprietorship, partnership, corporation or a joint-venture business which is at least 51 percent owned, operated and controlled by one or more people who are classified as a member of a minority group. In the case of a publicly owned business, in order to be classified as a minority-owned business, members of a minority group must own at least 51 percent of the business' stock. A minority group is a term used to define a group of people who hold few positions of power. Minority groups include African Americans, Asian American, Hispanic Americans, Native Americans and women. Minority-owned businesses must receive certification by city, state, or federal agencies in order to be classified as a minority-owned business.

WHAT IS A WOMEN BUSINESS ENTERPRISE

With specific regard to minority businesses owned by women, in order to be classified as a women-owned business, the business must demonstrate that the woman or women owners provide a contribution of capital and/or expertise in the business. The woman or women owners must also have control over management, policy, financial, and operational matters. The woman or women owners must also demonstrate self-sufficiency without reliance on another non-women-owned business for funding or resources.

MINORITY BUSINESS ENTERPRISES BY THE NUMBERS

In July 2010, the federal government released a report on the U.S. Census Bureau's 2007 Survey of Business Owners. The data in the report was collected as part of the 2007 Economic Census. The survey included a sample of more than 2.3 million nonfarm businesses filing 2007 tax forms as individual proprietorships, partnerships, or any type of corporation, and with receipts of $1,000 or more. Here are some findings from the study.

"Minority-owned businesses increased 45.5 percent from 2002 to 2007 from 4.0 million businesses to 5.8 million, while their receipts increased 55.0 percent. These minority-owned businesses accounted for 21.3 percent of the nation's businesses, employed 5.8 million persons (5.0 percent of the nation's employees) and generated $1.0 trillion in receipts (3.4 percent of the nation's receipts). Minority men-owned businesses numbered 2.9 million (10.7 percent of the nation's businesses), earning $710.8 billion in receipts (2.4 percent of the nation's receipts). Minority women-owned businesses numbered 2.2 million businesses (8.2 percent of the nation's businesses), earning $186.2 billion in receipts (0.6 percent of the nation's receipts). Minority-owned businesses that were equally owned by men and women accounted for 642,466 businesses (2.4 percent of the nation's businesses), earning $127.8 billion in receipts (0.4 percent of the nation's receipts)."

Source: Survey of Business Owners. Rep. United States Census Bureau, July 2010. Web. 10 July 2012.

<http://www.census.gov/econ/sbo/get07sof.html?18>

The federal government's Small Business Administration compiles a variety data on minority business enterprises in order to paint a picture of the status of minority-owned businesses across the United States.

"Minorities own 15.1% of all U.S. businesses, or more than 3 million firms, and 99% of these firms are small businesses."

Source: SBA, "Dynamics of Minority-Owned Employer Establishments, 1999-2001," February 2005

"Minority-owned businesses account for $591 billion in revenues."

Source: SBA, "Dynamics of Minority-Owned Employer Establishments, 1999-2001," February 2005

WOMEN BUSINESS ENTERPRISES BY THE NUMBERS

The Economics and Statistics Administration of the United States Department of Commerce released a report in October 2010 on women-owned businesses titled "Women Owned Businesses in the 21st Century." The report studied the changes in women-owned businesses over time, examined disparities in the characteristics of businesses owned by women as compared to those owned by men, and presented potential reasons for these disparities and the different outcomes that are associated with them. Here are some of the findings in the report.

- Women-owned businesses contribute significantly to the U.S. economy. In 2007, 7.8 million firms were owned by women, accounting for almost 30 percent of all non-farm, privately-held U.S. firms. Women-owned firms had sales/receipts of $1.2 trillion and those with paid employees had 7.6 million workers.

- The number of women-owned businesses has grown over time. Between 1997 and 2007, the number of women-owned businesses grew by 44 percent, twice as fast as men-owned firms and they added roughly 500,000 jobs while other privately held firms lost jobs. In part, this is because women-owned firms were more likely to be located in industry sectors that experienced employment growth, such as health care and education services.

- Between the years 1997 and 2002, the number of businesses owned by minority women increased faster than those owned by nonminority women, with minority women-owned firms accounting for more than half of the increase in women-owned businesses.

- Women-owned businesses are typically smaller than men-owned businesses. Although women own 30 percent of privately held businesses, these businesses account for only 11 percent of sales and 13 percent of employment among privately held companies. Average sales/receipts for women-owned businesses are only 25 percent of average sales/receipts for men-owned businesses. Women-owned businesses are concentrated in industry sectors where firms are typically smaller.

- There are substantial differences in the financing utilized by women-owned versus men-owned businesses. Women start with less capital than men and are less likely to take on additional debt to expand their businesses. They are more likely than men to indicate that they do not need any financing to start their business. It is difficult to distinguish preferences from constraints in these data. For instance, women may encounter less favorable loan conditions than men or they may be less willing to take on risk by seeking outside capital.

- The characteristics of self-employed women are similar to those of self-employed men. Compared to the non-self-employed, self-employed women and men are older, more likely to be married, and less likely to have children at home. However, women who are self-employed work fewer hours on average in their business than self-employed men.

- The annual earnings ratio between self-employed women and men is 55 percent, well below the ratio between non-self-employed women and men.

"Women-Owned Businesses in the 21st Century." Economics and Statistics Administration. United States Department of Commerce, 7 Oct. 2010. Web. 16 June 2012. <http://www.esa.doc.gov/Reports/women-owned-businesses-21st-century>.

WHAT IS MINORITY CERTIFICATION

Minority-owned business certification is a review process used to ensure a business is actually owned, controlled and operated by members of a minority group. Certification agencies are licensed by the government and perform the certification process on behalf of government entities and private institutions. The job of a certification agency is to verify that a business applying for minority certification meets the criteria required for certification.

There are a number of organizations that serve as resources for minority business owners. Once a minority business is certified, these organizations will aid them in gaining contracting opportunities. While there are organizations to aid minority businesses in building relationships with corporations, the federal government also has a number of programs to help minority-owned businesses acquire contracts.

NATIONAL MINORITY SUPPLIER DEVELOPMENT COUNCIL

The NMSDC provides a link between corporations and minority-owned businesses. The organization was chartered in 1972 to provide increased procurement and business opportunities for minority businesses of all sizes. Their network is made up of 3,500 corporate members, which includes the nation's largest publicly owned, privately-owned and foreign-owned companies, as well as universities, hospitals and other enterprises. The organization's members certified members total 16,000 minority-owned businesses. In 2010, the amount of purchases made by corporations in the NMSDC network totaled more than $100 billion. NMSDC has one national office and 37 regional councils throughout the country.

UNITED STATES SMALL BUSINESS ADMINISTRATION

The SBA serves as an advocate working to protect, strengthen and represent the interests of America's small businesses within the federal government. Under the banner of small businesses, the SBA provides certifications to minority-owned businesses through a variety of programs, including their Minority Business Development Agency. The SBA's minority certification program is focused on helping minority-owned businesses learn the criteria necessary to qualify as a minority-owned business. Since government agencies set aside contracts for businesses with this designation, the SBA works to educate minority-owned businesses on how certification gives them the ability to bid on and receive more government contracts.

HUB ZONE

The Historically Underutilized Business Zone Empowerment Contracting Program was created to stimulate economic development and create jobs in disadvantaged communities by providing federal contracting preferences to small businesses.

In order to be a part of the HUBZone program and receive designation as a HUBZone firm, a small business must be located in a "historically underutilized business zone," which are commonly found in urban and rural communities. Specifically, a "HUBZone" is an area that is located in an area designated by census data as a "non-metropolitan county." The Internal Revenue Code defines these areas according to the State median household income. Designated areas have a median household income of less than 80 percent or an unemployment rate of not less than 140 percent of the statewide average, which is determined based on the most recent data from the United States Department of Labor. These areas also include lands within the boundaries of federally recognized Indian reservations. An additional requirement is that a business must be owned and controlled by one or more United States citizens, and at least 35 percent of its employees must reside in a HUBZone.

In the HUBZone program, contracts are awarded as long as there is an evenhanded anticipation that a contract will be awarded at a fair market price and that at least two qualified HUBZone firms will bid on the contract. Special exceptions have been made to award contracts to singular small businesses. This is only permissible if there is not an expectation that two or more qualified small businesses will bid on the contract and that the government estimate will not exceed $5 million for manufacturing or $3 million for all other necessities. In the case of contracts requiring full and open competition, price related preferences might be given to small businesses. Small businesses that are certified as both Section 8(a) and HUBZone firms are eligible to qualify for additional preference points.

Often times minority business enterprises are located in the areas designated as HUBZones which means they are often the recipients of these contracts after they have applied and received their certification. However, in some instances minority-owned businesses have been denied certification for failing to meet the residential employee requirement. For those minority business enterprises seeking to receive HUBZone certification, there are resources available through the Minority Business Development Association.

SECTION 8(A) BUSINESS DEVELOPMENT PROGRAM

The section 8(a) business development program was developed to help socially and economically disadvantaged business owners. Through this program, these minority business enterprises, controlled or owned by a disadvantaged class are awarded federal agency contracts. In order to provide opportunities for disadvantaged minority business enterprises federal agencies are required to set aside contracts for section 8(a) certified business enterprises. Singular contract may also be granted to minority business enterprises in the case that the amount of the contract does not exceed $5 million for manufacturing requirements and $3 million for all other necessities.

In order to be admitted into the program a minority-owned business must be certified by SBA. Under federal law, specific groups are defined as socially disadvantaged. This definition includes the following groups: African Americans, Hispanic Americans, Asian Pacific Americans, Native Americans, and Subcontinent Asian Americans. Individuals who do not belong to these groups are still eligible to enter the program if they have evidence to demonstrate that they are disadvantaged because of race, ethnicity, gender, physical handicap, or residence in a social environment isolated from the conventional social norms.

Business enterprises wishing to be labeled as economically disadvantaged are required to demonstrate they have a net worth of less than the designated threshold determined by the government. This figure is calculated by excluding the value of the owner's business and personnel residence. Applicants are also required to meet designated size standards related to small businesses and have been in business for at least two years.

Businesses applying for admittance into the program must also demonstrate a rational capacity for success. This is an important component of the application process. In order to for the applicant to demonstrate they have the potential for success, the applicant must provide evidence to support the claim. According to the SBA this is defined as:

1. Access to credit and capital, including, but not limited to, access to long-term financing, access to working capital financing and bonding capability;

2. Technical and managerial experience of the applicant concern's managers, the operating history of the concern, the concern's record of performance; and

3. Requisite licenses if the concern is engaged in an industry requiring professional licensing.

In the instance that the applicant cannot demonstrate their capability, the MBE will not be certified for 8(a) participation.

Approximately 50 percent of minority business enterprises do not received 8(a) certification due to a lack of evidence supporting economic hardship or success capacity. Certification allows a minority owned business to participate in the program for up to nine years and remain certified as a small disadvantaged business for three years following the date of its last annual review.

HOW TO BECOME WOMEN-OWNED CERTIFIED

Women Business Enterprise National Council

According to the Women Business Enterprise National Council, in order to be certified as a women-owned business, a business must meet the following criteria:

"Applicant company must be at least fifty-one percent (51%) owned and controlled by one or more women who are U.S. citizens or lawful permanent residents, or in the case of any publicly-owned business, at least fifty-one percent (51%) of the equity of which is owned and controlled by one or more women who are U.S. citizens or lawful permanent residents; and whose management and daily operation is controlled by one or more of the women owners."

More than 1,000 corporations as well as institutions in a variety of states, cities and regions accept WBENC's certification. WBENC has also been granted the designation by the SBA as a Third Party Certifier for the Women-Owned Small Business Federal Contracting Program.

Here is the process of receiving certification as a women business enterprise according to WBENC:

"WBENC Certification validates that the business is 51 percent owned, controlled, operated, and managed by a woman or women. To achieve

WBENC Certification, women owned businesses complete a formal documentation and site visit process, which is administered by one of WBENC's 14 Regional Partner Organizations. WBENC Certification gives women owned businesses the ability to compete for real-time business opportunities provided by WBENC Corporate Members and government agencies.

1. A business entity submits an application, along with the necessary supporting documentation, notarized sworn affidavit and non-refundable processing fee.

2. Each RPO has a trained Certification Review Committee that meets on a monthly basis. Once the applicant's file is complete (meaning all documentation pertinent to the business and legal structure has been received), the application packet is reviewed by the Certification Review Committee.

3. An on-site visit is conducted at a pre-determined time with the majority woman business owner.

4. At a subsequent Certification Review Committee meeting, following the site visit, a final determination is made regarding the applicant's eligibility. ∘ If certification is granted, the company's owner and assigned contact will receive an automated-e-mail notification telling them that they have been certified and may now access their certificate online.

A formal letter is mailed to the owner if certification is denied.

SMALL BUSINESS ASSOCIATION

Women-owned business who have been certified by the WBENC or another certifying agency can take advantage of a number of contracting opportunity programs through the federal government. Regardless of a business' sizes or years of experience, certified women business enterprises are eligible to compete for the federal government's set-aside contracts. The federal government uses set-aside contracts in order to help them meet supplier diversity guidelines.

Women-owned businesses are also eligible to take advantage of the SBA's programs. Women business enterprises represent a large portion of the entities certified by the government's 8(a) and small disadvantaged business programs. They also represent a large portion of the companies who receive contracts and subcontract under the federal government's Department of Transportation's small and disadvantaged business program. In order to ensure the success of these programs, federal agencies are required to set contracting goals with women business enterprises and to set aside contracts in order to ensure these goals are met.

While certification as a women owned business is an important step to advancing a business, a women enterprise does not have to be formally certified in order to compete for prime contracts on federal procurements. The reason businesses do not have to be certified is because there are no preference programs for women-owned small businesses.

PROBLEMS

Problems sometimes arise when a minority or women owned business enterprise is going through the certification process. While the process of applying for certification can be somewhat arduous, it is important for applicants to follow the procedures set out by their certifying agencies. Those applicants who do not follow the appropriate procedure and provide all the necessary materials could find themselves denied certification.

One key problem is that in order to be certified, business owners must file a large amount of paperwork. This paperwork requires a wealth of information about the business owner personally along with their business. Some applications may also require owners to provide information on their families. While many business owners are familiar with the technical logistics of their operations, others might run a more informal business. In the case of the latter, a business owner might not have all of the required paperwork such as financial statements, licenses, and employee documentation. All of the required documentation must be provided in the application in order to ensure the process is not delayed.

The other key problem that arises during the application process is that applicants sometimes do not have the required evidence to support their identification as a minority or women business enterprise. In order to be certified, applicants must provide evidence verifying they meet the requirements of a minority or women business enterprise. Problems can arise when applicants are unable to prove that they are a majority owner of the business or have majority control over business decisions within the enterprise.

However, regardless of the problems that may arise during the process of applying for certification, the benefits of the certification are many.

Dr. Pamela Williamson: Women Business Enterprise Council - West

Dr. Pamela Williamson is the President of WBEC-West a regional partner of the Women's Business Enterprise National Council, a coalition of corporations, women business enterprises and women's business advocacy organizations. WBEC-West is responsible for implementing the certification standards of WBENC throughout Arizona, Colorado, Southern California, Utah, Wyoming, Nevada, Hawaii and Guam.

"Step one of certification is first to do your research to make sure certification fits within your business strategy of your corporation or company. The second step is once you've determined if that certification is right for you than you want to go on to the WBENC website and complete the online application.

Once you completed the online application, there's required documentation that you have to submit. The submitted documentation is reviewed by a Program Manager. Once that documentation has been reviewed and deemed to be fit to move forward than that file is sent to a certification committee. The certification committee is made up of individuals, either corporate representation community, corporations and community partners, MWBEs who will sit on the certification committee review and make recommendations whether your file is certifiable or not. After that determination is made then you're scheduled for a site visit. The site visitor will come out and do an independent review of your business and then make a recommendation. Those two recommendations are combined to determine whether you're certifiable or not certifiable. If you're certifiable you'll receive you certificate from the RPO. If you're not certified than as a potential WBE you have the right to file for an appeal. There's an appeals committee that will review your file. That determination is made. If you still feel the appeals committee did not understand your file for some reason or that you should be certified, than you have the right for a national appeal," Williamson said.

"The purpose of certification is to prove that you're 51 percent owned operated and controlled by a woman or women. Certification isn't a magic wand, but what it does do is get you a seat at the table. That seat could be removed at any time if you don't have the skills and ability and knowledge base to fulfill a contract or meet a need for a corporation. But what certification does is it allows you to sit at the table. It provides you access to corporations you have an advocate inside the organization. Supplier Diversity professionals are in those positions to be an internal advocate for you as a certified M/WBE. Certification provides you with an insider within corporations that are there knocking on doors and advocating on your behalf to make sure you always have a seat at the table when opportunities are present."

INCREASE YOUR OPPORTUNITY FOR SUCCESS

While obtaining certification as a minority or women-owned business is the first step to advancing a business toward success, utilizing the appropriate tools and resources is the key to ensuring a business gets the most out of certification. While certification is a necessary component for applying to government contracting opportunities, certification can also give businesses an edge in the corporate world.

More and more corporations are using certification to weed out applicants applying for their contracts. In a corporate supplier diversity program, corporations demonstrate their commitment to diversity by giving contracts to minority and women owned businesses. Certification is a way of ensuring these contracts go to actual minority and women owned businesses as opposed to a supplier pretending to be a minority or women owned business. So, while being a certified business will set a business apart from many of its competitors, many others will also have obtained certification to meet the demands of corporate buyers. Therefore it is necessary for diverse businesses to utilize tools and resources that can enhance their certification, set them apart from other diverse suppliers, and allow them to gain access to corporate contracting opportunities.

While there are a number of tools and resources available to women and minority owned businesses, some can be more beneficial than others. Among these tools and resources is Procurement Registration, a business intelligence platform that connects suppliers and buyers. While marketing is an important tool to promoting any business, gaining contracts require more than simply participating in trade shows and engaging both online and offline advertising.

In order to be successful, businesses must position themselves in front of buyers at the appropriate interval – when they are ready to buy. In order to be considered for contracting opportunities, minority and women owned businesses must register with a corporation's corporate portal. Since each corporation has their own registration system, it can be a complex and time consuming process to register with each prospective corporation. Businesses also waste time marketing their products and services to corporation with no potential to ever buy from them.

Procurement Registration simplifies the corporate buying portal registration process for suppliers and positions them to compete for contracting opportunities. Their system is a complete tool for small, medium, and large businesses. Their software is the only one on the market today that allows suppliers to complete one form and have their data automatically sent to all corporations with the click of a mouse.

The system allows users to view corporate profiles and gain access to business opportunities. Suppliers begin by uploading their information including business description, certifications, licenses, commodity codes and other pertinent information. This detailed business profile enables the system to create targeted qualified buyer matches. Their system also gives users access to contracting opportunities with local, state and federal agencies. Using their system, suppliers can search for opportunities and buyers by keyword, category, and other criteria.

Procurement Registration takes their registration and matching system to the next level by facilitating direct communication with buyers and category managers. Procurement Registration also enables the hosting of live meetings between buyers and suppliers.

As an industry leader in supplier diversity solutions, Procurement Registration provides buyers and suppliers with the technology to develop and sustain long-terms relationships. Procurement Registration's latest business intelligence platform simplifies matchmaking at buyer/supplier events. In addition to their registration system, they also help facilitate matchmaking events at conferences for minority and women owned businesses.

Procurement Registration has the only matchmaking system that allows vendors to register on a corporate portal with a click of a mouse. Their system verifies registration prior to making a match, instantly allowing corporations to see who meets their minimum requirements.

Their software analyses registered suppliers and creates face-to-face meeting appointments based on the corporation's and event's requirements. The system takes into account event length, the number of meeting tables, number of partner buyers attending, and individual buyer requirements.

Beyond Procurement Registration's software systems, they also offer users a variety of resources to advance their businesses and ensure they are informed and eligible to take advantage of contracting opportunities. Procurement Registration helps minority and women owned businesses refine and submit their capability statements. They also provide deep niche research on corporation including information on size, spending and more. Their users have access to a personal account assistant to help them get the most out of their subscription. In addition, users receive ongoing training and education from procurement experts.

Procurement Registrations offers several different plans to meet a variety of business sizes and budgets. With their system, minority and women owned businesses are matched with business opportunities from thousands of corporations throughout the United States, Canada, and around the globe. Their system is the perfect procurement solution for RFIs, RFPs, and RFUs. With their system, suppliers can shorten their sales cycle by placing their business in front of corporate buyers and category managers without creating additional work for the buyers.

TESTIMONIALS

Michelle Carnivalli: Gifford Electric Inc.

Even after a business receives certification as women business enterprise, it can still be difficult for women-owned businesses to get their foot in the door.

Michelle Carnivalli is part owner of Gifford Electric Inc., a full service contractor who has served the commercial and industrial business of Las Vegas since 1959. Her company provides services in electrical, computer power, cabling and fiber optics to meet the electrical power and communication needs of their clients.

Carnivalli had been in business for a few years before she decided to pursue registration with a large vendor. However, when she began to pursue registration with the vendor, she found the process was more difficult than she had anticipated.

"I had been a women-owned business for a couple of years and I attempted to get registered with a large vendor. The person I was in communication with really discouraged me from doing that. He basically used statements like, 'well you can register with us, but we really don't have any work for you at this time so it's kind of a waste of time.' He said, things like that, things that were discouraging. I had tried to submit information that he requested and then he would come back and say that he wanted everything in one email instead of several emails, just things that made it

25

harder. I just felt discouraged through the whole process," Carnivalli said

It wasn't until she attended a women's business conference that she finally gained the tools and the knowledge she needed to gain registration with the vendor she previously pursued.

"Then last year I attended a women-owned business conference and was actually able to meet the diversity department representative for that same company at the conference. At that point we started communicating and I explained to her my discouragement with the previous attempt. She actually told me who I needed to contact, got me all set up and when it was time to submit the information to that same person that I originally worked with, the process went quite smoother. There were no discouraging comments at that point. I was registered within a couple of weeks, after submitting everything again and the process went a lot smoother," Carnivalli said.

From this experience, Carnivalli learned the importance of building relationships with supplier diversity managers. She also learned the importance of attending conferences for women business owners and the wealth of knowledge that can be gained from them.

"There was a very good benefit to working with the diversity division and to attending the conference of my women-owned business council as well. The woman I talked to, actually also gave me a lead that was for some work in another part of Nevada that there was no way I would've known about that work without that lead. It was a contract that I'm assuming had been set aside for a women-owned business, and that's why she was even looking for someone to fill that slot. So I had that lead, and I wouldn't have had that opportunity otherwise," Carnivalli said.

Leslie Janeen: Janeen LLC

Leslie Janeen is the owner of Janeen LLC, a management services company. Janeen was first inspired to have her business certified as a women business enterprise when she began getting involved with the Women Business Enterprise Council.

"There are many reasons that I want to have certification. It originated because I was introduced to the Women Business Enterprise Council and I wanted to become part of it. It is filled with dynamic women and men that are successful entrepreneurs, corporations, all walks of life and all working with the common goal of bringing business and synergy together under one umbrella for the purpose of diversity and I think that when you do that it speaks volumes. I believed in that from the beginning of being introduced to it," Janeen said.

For Janeen, the value of WBEC was not only measured by the organization's potential for advancing her company. She was also attracted to WBEC because of the social relationships she could build and because of her personal commitment to promoting diversity.

"On a personally professional level the network and the relationships that I'm going to make is going to empower and enrich my life and my business, beyond reason. I'm looking forward to lifelong friends and lifelong clients and a network. And just really having skin in the game from a business and personal perspective, becoming involved as a volunteer, I strive to work at all of those levels. From a business perspective, I look to achieve business at contracting and bid levels that perhaps I would not have been eligible for or would not have been easy to attain, if I did not have this certification," Janeen said.

After Janeen became certified with WBEC she began to immediately see the benefits of the certification. Being certified by WBEC allowed her to expand her business and take advantage of greater opportunities.

"My belief in the certification was immediate and I have worked tirelessly for the past year. While I have stumbled, I stumbled for the first 6 months because I was so caught up in being overwhelmed and while I play in the field of some of those big corporations in the business I do, my business itself is not. So that tripped me up at times. But I got past it. The people that work within the organization are so kind and generous in their assistance and in their encouragement and in the resources that they give whether it's people or networking or what have you that once I got passed that, I realized that there is a place for everyone just like in diversity. I do believe that this certification can mean the future success of Janeen LLC; that's how strongly I feel," Janeen said.

Robin and Marian Heymsfield: Zorbitz

In 2003, mother daughter team Marian and Robin Heymsfield conceived the idea for Zorbitz, a line of inspirational jewelry and charms that promotes good luck, love, peace, and happiness. Nearly a decade later, their products are distributed around the globe. Often times, certification as a minority or women enterprise is all a business needs to take them to the next level.

"We have about 200 reps around the country that sell our products. We have distributors all over. We sell all over the world. We sell in France, Australia, Germany, and Canada," Robin Heymsfield said.

"Basically we sell really great gemstones, beautiful gemstones, and beautiful crystals at affordable prices. That's what we believe in. We hope this inspires other people to say 'you can,'" said Marian Heymsfield.

Deanna Edwards: IntuCorporation

Deanna Edwards is the founder and president of IntuCorporation, a massage therapy services company. From starting out as a one-property service in Mississippi for the 1999 World Poker Open, Edwards has used her women business enterprise certification to expand her company to several hotels in Las Vegas.

"I've been very fortunate and very blessed with what I'm doing and the direction that my company and my life has gone from 1999 to now. I ate slept and worked, and did massage. For a year in a half that's all I did. When I first got to Las Vegas, I was only at the Bellagio Poker Room and now currently we provide massage therapy service at Bellagio Mirage, Mandalay Bay, MGM in Las Vegas, and then we provide massage services to the Beau Rivage and the Gold Strike in Mississippi."